MW01620673

Tosca's Paris Adventure

www.toscasparisadventure.com

ISBN 978-0-9785415-0-7

Printed in China

Book design by Lesley Gasparetti and Tania Baban
First Hardbound Edition

CONFLU:X PRESS
P.O. Box 12445
Marina del Rey, CA 90295
www.confluxpress.com

Written and Illustrated by

ABBY WASSERMAN

Poire and Poireau have just arrived on holiday in Paris with their cat, Tosca.

On their first morning they enjoy croissants and café au lait at a sidewalk café. Poireau gives Tosca warm milk in a saucer.

They look for antiques at the flea market. Poire buys a pair of candlesticks and Tosca chooses a small blue china cat.

They visit a grand museum and sit on its fountain, enjoying the sun. Tosca meets a dog. Although he is friendly, she's glad he's on a leash.

At the flower shop, Tosca meets a cat named Basho. He doesn't live with the flower seller, but is always welcome to visit.

Basho invites Tosca to a puppet show. She thinks she'll be back before Poire and Poireau notice she is gone.

The new friends pass a shop where meat and cheese are sold. A pair of street musicians are playing, but unfortunately, the cats have no time to stop and listen.

The puppet show in the park has begun! It is the dramatic story of a prince and a princess. Tosca and Basho are entranced.

Basho, who has lived in Paris since he was a kitten, leads Tosca onto a tower high above the trees.

Poire and Poireau look for the missing Tosca. They call and call, but she does not come.

ST. POIREAU
STE POIRE
ST. CHAT

Basho shows Tosca
the stained glass windows
in a great cathedral.
She admires their colors and
the carved wooden arches
below. They climb a long
spiral staircase to the roof.

The sunset is beautiful. As it begins to get dark, Tosca asks to return to the hotel, but the door to the stairway is locked!

Night falls, and dreadful creatures come out to stare at them. A hard bright ring circles the moon.

Feeling Basho will protect her, Tosca gradually loses her fear and falls asleep. The sky dances with brilliant stars.

Poire, very worried, has cried herself to sleep. Poireau sits up most of the night.

MÉMOIRE PERDUE
PARIS
CHATS PERDUS

In the morning they go to the police station, where Sergeant Haricot, Chief of the Lost Cats section, shows them photographs of cats who were brought in during the night. Tosca is not among them.

Madame
Patat'douce
VOYANTE
MEDIUM

Sergeant Haricot brings Poire and Poireau to his friend Madame Patat'douce, the famous fortune teller. She has found many lost cats in the past. Noiro, the raven who can see great distances, is ready to help, as is Emeraude, the lizard.

The crystal ball clears to reveal the two cats. "That is my Basho," exclaims the fortune teller, "so naughty, always running away! But I fear they are in danger. We must go quickly!"

The cats are indeed in danger. A fierce dog called Toro has driven Tosca into a box and is barking at her. Basho jumps up and down, trying to divert his attention.

Tosca bravely confronts Toro. "Is this how you treat visitors to your country?" she demands.

"I just wanted you to run so I could chase you," the big dog says meekly. He calls his friends Roux and Dan, who join them.

The dogs have many questions about America. Toro asks what games dogs play there. "Fetch the stick," Tosca says. "Catch the ball." "It's the same here," the dogs agree.

Here come the rescuers! Emeraude rides on the fortune teller's cap and Noiro flies overhead.

Poire and Poireau scold Tosca for leaving without a word, and Madame Patat'douce speaks sternly to Basho. The dogs, who also went out to play without telling anyone, creep guiltily home.

Tosca sadly watches her friend Basho go with Madame Patat'douce, Emeraude and Noiro. Poire, Poireau and Tosca are next to depart. They thank the kind Sergeant Haricot, who is the last to leave.

Poire and Poireau talk for hours as Tosca sleeps. How to make sure she doesn't get lost again? Paris is such a big city, and Tosca is so small...

Tosca is proud of her new red balloon and Poire and Poireau are happy with their solution. As they browse for books along the river, Tosca thinks about Basho and their adventure together. She hopes he can see her pretty balloon floating on the wind.

The End

TOSCA'S PARiS ADVENTURE

Poire and Poireau have just arrived on holiday in Paris with their cat, Tosca. On their first morning they enjoy croissants and café au lait at a sidewalk café. Poireau gives Tosca warm milk in a saucer.

They look for antiques at the flea market. Poire buys a pair of candlesticks and Tosca chooses a small blue china cat.
They visit a grand museum and sit on its fountain, enjoying the sun.
Tosca meets a dog. Although he is friendly, she's glad he's on a leash.

At the flower shop, Tosca meets a cat named Basho. He doesn't live with the flower seller, but is always welcome to visit.
Basho invites Tosca to a puppet show. She thinks she'll be back before Poire and Poireau notice she is gone.

The new friends pass a shop where meat and cheese are sold. A pair of street musicians are playing, but unfortunately, the cats have no time to stop and listen.
The puppet show in the park has begun! It is the dramatic story of a prince and a princess. Tosca and Basho are entranced.

Basho, who has lived in Paris since he was a kitten, leads Tosca onto a tower high above the trees.
Poire and Poireau look for the missing Tosca. They call and call, but she does not come.

Basho shows Tosca the stained glass windows in a great cathedral.
She admires their colors and the carved wooden arches below.
They climb a long spiral staircase to the roof.

L'AVENTURE DE TOSCA À PARiS

Poire et Poireau viennent d'arriver en vacances à Paris avec leur chat Tosca.
Le premier matin, en terrasse d'un café, ils savourent des croissants et du café au lait. Tosca a droit à un peu de lait chaud dans une soucoupe que lui donne Poireau.

Il vont au marché aux puces pour chercher des antiquités. Poire achète une paire des chandeliers, Tosca, lui, choisit un petit chat bleu en porcelaine.
Ils visitent un impressionnant musée puis, s'assoient au bord d'une fontaine en profitant du soleil. Tosca recontre un chien. Bien qu'il ait l'air gentil, elle préfère le savoir en laisse.

Chez la fleuriste, Tosca rencontre un chat qui s'appelle Basho. Il n'habite pas avec la fleuriste mais y est toujours le bievenue.
Basho invite Tosca à un spectacle de marionnettes. Elle pense être revenue avant que Poire et Poireau ne s'aperçoivent de son absence.

Les nouveaux amis passent devant une charcuterie-fromagerie. Des musiciens jouent dans la rue, mais malheureusement, les chats n'ont pas le temps de s'arrêter pour écouter.
Le spectacle de marionnettes dans le parc commence! Il s'agit d'une histoire passionnante entre un prince et une princesse. Tosca et Basho sont émerveillés.

Basho, qui vit à Paris depuis qu'il est chaton, emmène Tosca sur une tour bien plus haute que les arbres.
Poire et Poireau cherchent Tosca. Ils l'appellent sans cesse mais elle ne vient pas.

Basho montre à Tosca les vitraux d'une magnifique cathédrale. Elle admire leurs couleurs ainsi que les voûtes en bois sculpté.
Ils grimpent un escalier en colimasson jusqu'au toit.

The sunset is beautiful. As it begins to get dark, Tosca asks to return to the hotel, but the door to the stairway is locked!
Night falls, and dreadful creatures come out to stare at them. A hard bright ring circles the moon.

Le coucher de soleil est magnifique. Lorsqu'il commence à faire sombre, Tosca demande à rentrer à l'hôtel, mais la porte de l'escalier est fermée.
La nuit tombe, et des créatures effrayantes surgissent et les regardent fixement. La lune est encerclée d'un anneau de lumière dure.

Feeling Basho will protect her, Tosca gradually loses her fear and falls asleep. The sky dances with brilliant stars.
Poire, very worried, has cried herself to sleep. Poireau sits up most of the night.

Comme Tosca sent que Basho la protègera, sa crainte finit par s'envoler et elle s'endort. Le ciel danse avec des étoiles scintillantes.
Poire, très inquiète, s'est endormie en pleurant. Poireau reste éveillé presque toute la nuit.

In the morning they go to the police station, where Sergeant Haricot, Chief of the Lost Cats section, shows them photographs of cats who were brought in during the night. Tosca is not among them.

Le lendemain matin ils se rendent au poste de police, où le Sergent Haricot, Chef du département des chats perdus, leur montre des photos de chats trouvés pendant la nuit. Mais Tosca n'en fait pas partie.

Sergeant Haricot brings Poire and Poireau to his friend Madame Patat'douce, the famous fortune teller. She has found many lost cats in the past. Noiro, the raven who can see great distances, is ready to help, as is Emeraude,the lizard.
The crystal ball clears to reveal the two cats. "That is my Basho," exclaims the fortune teller, "so naughty, always running away! But I fear they are in danger. We must go quickly."

Sergent Haricot conduit Poire et Poireau chez son amie Madame Patat'douce, la célèbre voyante. Elle a déjà permis de retrouver beaucoup de chats perdus auparavant. Noiro, le corbeau capable de voir à de très grandes distances, est prêt à les aider, tout comme Emeraude, le lézard.
La boule de cristal devient claire et revélé deux chats.
- «C'est mon Basho,» s'exclame la voyante. -«Le vilain, toujours en train de s'enfuir ! Mais je crains qu'ils ne soient en danger !»

The cats are indeed in danger. A fierce dog called Toro has driven Tosca into a box and is barking at her. Basho jumps up and down, trying to divert his attention.

Les chats sont effectivement en danger. Un chien menaçant appellé Toro, a poursuivi Tosca jusque dans un carton et la guette en aboyant.
Basho sautille dans tous les sens, pour attirer l'attention de Toro.

Tosca bravely confronts Toro. "Is this how you treat visitors to your country?" she demands.
"I just wanted you to run so I could chase you," the big dog says meekly. He calls his friends Roux and Dan, who join them.
The dogs have many questions about America. Toro asks what games dogs play there. "Fetch the stick," Tosca says. "Catch the ball." "It's the same here," the dogs agree.

Tosca affronte bravement Toro: - «Est-ce ainsi que vous traitez ceux qui visitent votre pays ?» - «Je voulais juste te faire courir pour que je puisse te poursuivre,» dit le gros chien, tout penaud. Il appelle ses amis Roux et Dan, qui les rejoignent. Les chiens ont plein de questions à propos de l'Amérique. Toro demande à quoi jouent les chiens là-bas.
- «Ramener le baton,» dit Tosca. - «Attrapper la balle.»
- «C'est la même chose ici,» disent les chiens.

Here come the rescuers! Emeraude rides on the fortune teller's cap and Noiro flies overhead.
Poire and Poireau scold Tosca for leaving without a word, and Madame Patat'douce speaks sternly to Basho. The dogs, who also went out to play without telling anyone, creep guiltily home.

Voici les secouristes ! Emeraude voyage sur le chapeau de la voyante, et Noiro vole au-dessus d'eux.
Poire et Poireau disputent Tosca pour être partie sans les prévenir, et Madame Patat'Douce parle sévèrement à Basho. Les chiens qui eux aussi sont sortis jouer sans prévenir personne, rentrent en rasant les murs.

Tosca sadly watches her friend Basho go with Madame Patat'douce, Emeraude and Noiro. Poire, Poireau and Tosca are next to depart. They thank the kind Sergeant Haricot, who is the last to leave.
Poire and Poireau talk for hours as Tosca sleeps. How to make sure she doesn't get lost again? Paris is such a big city, and Tosca is so small...

Tosca regarde tristement son ami Basho s'en-aller avec Madame Patat'Douce, Emeraude et Noiro. Poire, Poireau et Tosca partent ensuite. Ils remercient le bon Sergent Haricot, qui est le dernier a partir.
Poire et Poireau discutent pendant des heures, tandis que Tosca dort. Comment s'assurer qu'elle ne se perde plus ? Paris est une si grande ville et Tosca est si petite...

Tosca is proud of her new red balloon and Poire and Poireau are happy with their solution. As they browse for books along the river, Tosca thinks about Basho and their adventure together. She hopes he can see her pretty balloon floating on the wind.

The End

Tosca est fière de son nouveau ballon rouge, et Poire et Poireau sont contents de leur solution. Alors qu'ils parcourent les bouquinistes le long du fleuve, Tosca repense à ses aventures avec Basho. Elle espère qu'il voit son beau ballon flottant dans le vent.

Fin

French translation by Aurélie A. Vincent

Traduit de l'anglais par Aurélie A. Vincent

GLOSSARY:

Poire (*pwahr*) – Pear

Poireau (*pwahr-oh*) – Leek

Croissant (*cwa-son*) – Buttery French pastry

Café au lait (*cah-fay-oh-lay*) – Steamed milk with espresso

Hôtel Légume (*oh-tell lay-goom*) – Vegetable Hotel

Chats Perdus (*shah payr-doo*) – Lost Cats

Mémoire Perdue (*mem-wahr payr-doo*) – Lost Memory

Sergent Haricot (*sir-jon ah-ree-coh*) – Sergeant Green Bean

Madame Patat'Douce – (*mah-dahm paw-tawt-doos*) – Madam Sweet Potato

Voyante Médium (*voy-an med-yum*) – Fortune Teller

Noiro (*nwar-oh*) – Blackie

Emeraude *(em-rowd)* – Emerald

Toro (*toh-roh*) – Bull (Spanish)

Roux (*roo*) – Rusty

FAMOUS PLACES IN THE STORY:

The Pyramid at the Louvre Museum – La Pyramide du Louvre

The Eiffel Tower – La Tour Eiffel

Nôtre Dame Cathedral – La Cathédrale Nôtre Dame

The shore of the Seine River – La rive de la Seine

For Josh and Allison, Graham and Bronwen, William and Nicholas.

Abby Wasserman lives in Mill Valley, California, with her husband, Potter Wickware. Her whimsical characters are based on family members and their beloved cats.